Experiential Adventures

LESLEY CLARY SAGE

Experiential Adventures.

ISBN - 978-1-8381149-3-0

First Published in 2021 by the Soulful Group

We unlace words & detangle life to help make the world a more soulful place.

www.soulfulgroup.com

Cover photography by Anthony Modinos
Cover design by Soulful Group
Dedication page art by Andy Frost
Interior art sourced via Canva

Experiential Adventures

Experiential Adventures encapsulates delightful shimmering wordplay, giving the reader much pause for thought. Lesley's poems are finely observed with a sensuous subtlety. There is a sure footedness to the composition, the music of her words if you will. They offer threads of different images to follow, both pleasingly discursive and tenable. No doubt readers will enjoy, be immersed, and much rewarded by her poetry as much as I have.

Carol Leeming MBE FRSA | Poet & Playwright

Experiential Adventures is a window into Lesley's soul and delves deep into the rich tapestry and magic of existence – of the unknown and the unseen. Her lyrical potency takes you on a dance, infusing a myriad connection of the senses. It is about beauty, often amidst pain and normality, projected through the eyes, experiences, and wisdom of a sage. Inspired by vision, Experiential Adventures is a rapturous journey in mystical poetry that imbues your imagination and touches your soul.

Richard C. Bower | Journalist & Poet

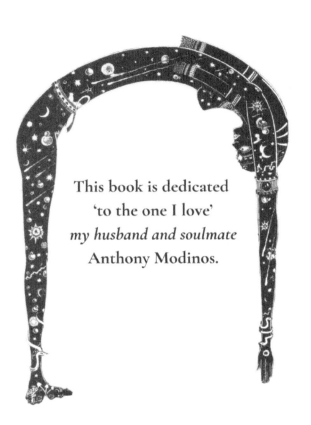

This book is dedicated
'to the one I love'
my husband and soulmate
Anthony Modinos.

Acknowledgements

Thank you, first and foremost to my beloved husband Tony Modinos for supporting me and our many projects and festivals over the years. Andy Frost for the dedication page artwork. My family especially Pat, Jean, Sera and Josie, Anne and Marie for their incredible patience and help throughout troublesome times as well as creating and sharing all those good times. Carol Leeming MBE FRSA for her positive mentoring and inspiring talent, so generously giving her time, friendship, and attention. Shobana and the team at Soulful Group, who have been so patient, understanding, and helpful throughout the process of bringing 'Experiential Adventures' into being. All those in Tangent Poetry, Soundswrite and Western Words for helping shape and improve my words, as well as Leicester Inter Faith and all you many Guides to life.

Time flies over us but leaves its shadow behind —

- Nathaniel Hawthorne

1. TIMELESS

1. HARMONIC CONVERGENCE
2. TIME IS A CRIME OF PASSION
3. BINDING SPELL
4. INSTINCTIVE
5. WALKING ON THE WHEEL OF THE GREEN DAWN
6. CLIFFTOP VIEW
7. MOUNTAIN FIRE
8. SONG SHAPERS
9. EAST
10. SOUTH
11. ABERTREWEREN BACK DOOR VIEW
12. BUZZ
13. FELL WALK
14. CROFT HILL
15. IMAGINE A FOREST
16. SCRUMPING IN SID'S GARDEN
17. CANAL TRIP
18. CASTLE GARDENS
19. IMBOLC TO MAYDAY BREAKING THROUGH
20. AUBADE
21. DEMENTIA TEST

1. HARMONIC CONVERGENCE

A sigh between two mysteries
birth the intent
death completion.
Breathe the song of the world
as she splinters into separate perception.
Love is the purpose, the healing
joining each to each and us to we,
a changing kaleidoscope
of patternings in the void
given human form as we meet
and meld in pairs, groups, gatherings
giving, taking all that's needed
to shape the song of the world.
Sing of the sigh between two mysteries
Life's pleasure and pain.

2. TIME IS A CRIME OF PASSION

Time is a crime of passion
visited upon us by the jealous
Angels of go-between, to show
the spoiling of a perfect state of grace
by growth and entropy.
Those halfway beings of precious essence
beyond the reach of conscious mind
force us from endless bliss and knowing not,
into the joy of Winter day's snowdrop,
bird cry, lion's roar, grandchild's smile,
'til the developed mind stays,
learning to live in the moment,
"concedes to time, inch by inch".
That one togetherness with all and me
that really makes all else forgotten
and apart, falls away.
We become beguiled with the dancing skyhorses,
with the form of beauty and the sound of waves,
the taste of freedom and individual.
We touch another and become
born to pain, joy and glory.
The all is briefly glimpsed, joined
so long ago and now
experienced so rarely,
we call it gone, the Paradise, God, Goddess.
That eternity of bliss and merge,
(not I but everything and one)
we fell from, pushed by jealous
sister / brother / cuckoo fledglings
into a timeline of here, now, was,
will be again.

Time is a crime
of passion, we only record and regret.

3. BINDING SPELL

Bound with chains of midnight silver
Mithrael gleam in darkest void dance,
spiral strings of starlight in the hopeless
gloom of night's despair, trace convoluted
pathways through the fearsome mazement.
Labyrinthine knowledge of our doom
offer us guidance and truesight light.

Mindseye sight etched deep in soulshine
meld our boundaries of auric power,
from deep reach within to fullest soulstretch
biting hard into the core of knowing,
taste the bloodprice of the binding
looped crystal nets, diamond edged,
woven from flames of passion and desire.

Bound with brightest burning noon gold,
which reddened hue adorns the bold
insistent greed of always lovers,
as the sun rises on our promises,
as the sun sets on our dreams.
Golden haze of truesight, hold us tight.
Warmth of growing. Entwined the prize.

4. INSTINCTIVE

When real is touch and hold and heal,
no distancing, just singing
all else is merely incident
whilst conspiring, realigning
to the said world, to the ephemeral.
The world that freely I frequent,
borne on musics, traced in storm,
is warmed, infused, all disabused
of meanings; accepting is
and this and us, held enthralled
for moments longer than held form.
Eternal carvings in the void,
whittled, woven into karmic strands
that bind our souls as one with all,
no distancing, just singing
when real is touch and hold and heal.

5. WALKING ON THE WHEEL OF THE GREEN DAWN

Breezing toward the dawn,
at that place of melding, melting
in the green shimmering of earthly reach,
toward that freshest moment,
where translucent buds,
unfolding leaves, suffused with lightness
of new born world, in daybreak's breeze
are tossed toward the warming sun
from still held night and calm begun,
healing wounds of blockage.
Stiffened weary limbs of grope and grasp,
in blind tracery of power and form,
become a bursting free chaos of
sprouting growth, from labrynthined
ordered sleep. The base and deep
rootedness of being, to highest reach
in the now known multiversal patternings
of choice.
So stars are born, intrusive light becomes
the pearl of knowledge.
Change, true treasure, treasured.
Difference, love makes true, infused,
the rule and knowledge, alchemy.
Shared epiphany of that bright piercing
zephyred touch of spinning season.

6. CLIFFTOP VIEW

Foam flecks, like mating butterflies, flutter up the cliff,
dancing in the gusty gusting arms of air, whilst seagulls
fiercely battle with the wind to produce stillness,
effortless static
born of subtle changes of wingtip, gasping angles, riffled
feathers.
Waves following the wind, skipping and bobbing, leaping
in eagerness for the very tiplets of frothy veil
to see the end of the journey. They caress the shore,
part and splinter, then shelter against the serpentine
edges of cruel jewelshards,
carpetting in whipped frenzied daring, to make the
change
from ever shifting into now and left behind.
Solid definite beauty, static rock.

7. MOUNTAIN FIRE

I hold my hand to my eyes,
seeing fingers and palm dissolve
into whirling atoms and galaxies,
the fire crackling and illuming
night sky, crowded trees.
The high ground falling to a
deep dark valley, hidden below
dryads and green beings dance.
The cosmos wheeled and became
all one in feeling the night,
my soul leaping forth, melding
to the everything of all.
I could smell the acrid trail of fox, smoke,
hear the snuffle of badger
eating in the undergrowth,
hear the worms munching grass down, rustling.
I was the worm chewing through the world,
the dirt between the spaces.
I felt the solid earth melt beneath
and floated through space
spinning with the universe.
Grounded on the earth with
Jack O'Lantern guiding the way
through to the very tip
of being, one with all,
whilst other humans slept.

8. SONG SHAPERS

The spiral runs arush the swirl again,
catch it on the crest
froth the wave and cast
the weave into a web,
to catch the moon, beam.
Sun comes, air moves, earth dreams,
whistling dust along the road
whirling dervish schemes
spinning senseless meanings,
into everyday a sense of all the new.
Turn of the screw.
Scorching wind to flame the sky
consume the growth, burn the earth
in fiery glow of sunset.
In the darkness cracking cold and fire within,
feel the crystal edge,
of just a step beyond.
Feel the burning void
of misplaced footing
see the moonglow.
Catch the spiral as she turns to shed the ash and slime
of those who missed the ride.

9. EAST

Sit here in that gleam between
darkness and sunbegun,
conjure strengths to shape the day,
turn towards that first seen,
a place of breaking hope
as it lights the real world.
A trotting streak, camouflaged
gold red sunbeam, cunning,
crafty, he steals toward
still sleeping birds, pounces, bites,
desperate flapping wings,
bite hard, taste gush blood, bite.
Drop the prize, search for more,
take what is, before
two legs, noisy, screech, swish, zoom,
can catch up. Prize mouthed
careful into safe, tended place.
Shelter from eyes, smells known
of old enemy and fresh kill.
Tasty licks, bone and soft meat
left out, stale two legs smell, regular.
Tear covering off not now flying things,
scatter the grass with signs of prowess,
eat bones, head and flesh, crunch crunch,
spray the edges of place,
(smell strong of mighty hunter)
claim space. Then camouflage, tricksy,
cunning, trots back to sleep space,
wait for between time again.
Listening for dogs, diggers,
two legs not in zoom screech.

10. SOUTH

Place of warm breeze promise of Spring,
see the soaring gimlet-eyed quarter the ground,
looking for roadkill, shot and downed,
smaller fluttering's and scuttering's,
grass trails and ripened crops,
anywhere attracting those that can be eaten.
Sparkles of light reflected from plumage, water,
stranded pond life and incautious worms
seeking the promise of a dry day.
Swoop, clutch, screech, perch and tear.
Spurt of blood staining breast and beak,
hooding the prize from coveting eyes.
Focus on the easy meat, cast off the outer cover,
pull down the soft and squidgy meat,
pull down with bloody talons the corpse and feast.
Up again for the mate waiting at nest,
quarter the ground, looking for roadkill,
shot and downed, fluttering's and scuttering's,
until the land grows dark and it's time to rest.
Purpose renewed with the dawn.

11. ABERTREWEREN BACK DOOR VIEW

On the bank beneath the trees
daffodils, dancing, weave their way
to stretch and reach towards the
distant view of other valley side,
as though the very intent and bobbing grace
could seed the faraway high horizon.
The patchwork greenery brightened, lightened
underneath the tree gloom standings
by the golden trumpeting, all attention,
leaning forward, glowing in the breeze.
Glittering green companion leaves
supporting the advance into perception,
gently apart from the crowded bramble,
yet near enough to every guardian tree
for each bright bunch to feel
the ancient security of planted
deep footings in the lee of aged rock.
Steep bank, with solitary bumble bee
creating harmonies.

12. BUZZ

Buzzz
Bee falls
To leaf litter
Antennae waving
Greetings, climbs onto hand.
Offering skin hold, arm length
A way from bird, cold rain, fierce wind,
Towards shelter, warmth and honey drop.
Three days she rests, explores around, remains
Content, exercises her wings, stretched, leapt
From stony height to bluebells and moss
Contained in bell jar, sunwarmed, safe.
Then, ready or not tries, flies,
Buzzes to leave, go home.
Taken on handhold,
Given a choice,
Leaf litter,
Burrows
Buzzz.

13. FELL WALK

Gush of water as it was gulped
and gargled into the crevices
and runnel tunnels along the fell (in)
banks of sweet turf. Sphagnum moss,
moorland flowers sparkled in the sun,
tiny yellow cross petals, with leaves
so small spiked the sun couldn't stroke
a way in between them.
Cotton candy fluffed grasses
clouded the reed bed, dark damp glistening
at their footings, whilst higher
scrambling the red and spring green
bilberries seemingly took themselves
on flights of fancied flutterby
as gatherings of matings dipped and swirled.
Far away above the ridge and fringed crest
of skymeet and treereach
gaudy hang glidings tried to match
the freedom of the breeze.

14. CROFT HILL

Sweet surging to the very top of kite fly,
Quarry edge and fall,
vistas of low-lie, occasional heights
in Leicester realms,
contrast with rock-bite, rubble strewn
Earth rape for flat roads in a flattened land.
Think, no more rising from the everyday
into the sunset, to peak over rim
at the coming dawn.
No views but nearby.
No out of breath with quickened gasp of wonder
as turning toward the fall away,
kite flies, even beyond the touched sky.
No picnics, sat with head in clouds,
no turf roll, nor lay down,
no dreaming at quiet day,
listening to lark song.
Croft Hill may disappear,
be strewn throughout the land,
rocks distressed, disturbed and crushed,
that once was bedrock, toe hold,
as we climbed and ran,
playing with kites at the end of the world.

15. IMAGINE A FOREST

Imagine a forest on a hot summer's day,
sheltering life, from the dappled leaf litter
to the highest eyrie of the osprey.
Open glades for bluebells, grasses, rabbits, deer.
Oak with three thousand lifeforms standing alone.
Beech, ash and lime spreading the canopy,
shades of green,
shading out seedlings in their race to the sun.
Constant buzzing of insects, bird calls echoing.
Bees, wasps and squirrels, badgers, the fox.
Imagine the acorns, nuts and fruits
dropping as manna, eaten, spread.
Imagine the boltholes beneath the roots
sheltering life from birth to death.
Imagine the streams rushing along
from steep tumble beginnings of watery song,
cut deep ravine, slow winding river valley,
and always the trees, deep on the banks,
mounting steep horizon, soaring in ranks.
All combined more than the whole,
delight for eyes and soaring soul.
Imagine the whole, soft smells, textured touch,
a place of sanctuary gifted for us.
Imagine it gone.

16. SCRUMPING IN SID'S GARDEN

We feasted in Sid's Garden,
red currants, blackberries, gooseberry and tay,
raspberry and roses, roses all the way,
earth banks bounded the distance to the sky,
hedgeling and brambling roaming by.
Sweeps of sweet grasses, meadow hay and flowers,
spiralled carved out contours, timeless hours.
Pools of living movement, sky summer blue,
drifts of waving foliage, colours peeping through,
euphoric butterflies trace danced in grace,
as we stepped through the shared sacred space.
The buddleia's heady breath mingled with the rest,
we feasted in delight, sun turned to west.
Greedy city children, cherry picking country delight,
then the seen in Sid's eye, future growth and sharing,
caring for the land, peaceful waves of happy home,
so we can understand, the pleasure of an afternoon.
Not dreaming, in the garden.

17. CANAL TRIP

Sunshine blossoms on the water
bird flies by,
inquisitive eagle eyed
others in a hazy afternoon
reach out their hands,
offerings to friendship, well met
and help along the way.
Cruise time day
easing into slip, steady
once tied tight banks
gentle bumping, repulsing.

Watched over, reflect upon
the rippling trees, the early evening
breath of bathed in setting sun
between the to and from.
Mirrored through the dappling
glance on water, shine in eyes
blindingly over the edge
rising at majick angles
slabbed stone, steep stepped,
locked into a time of wait
and seeing others wind along.

Time measured in the slow rise
and soft fall, sudden surgings
sweet sweep of foaming.
Above us only skylined shadows
silhouettes against a bluesome sky,
shadows dancing, locked against wet walls
whilst waterfalling into calm, collected.

Spindrifted into curtainings
hung upon a roped height, held tight
made for drifting, floating, dream rising.
Shifting sway to changed routine.

18. CASTLE GARDENS

A footfall from temple ring,
a body throw from head and heel bridge,
where between the Union and the Soar
the presence of Mithrais and the slandered king
weaves bright unlikely days into the common place,
before stepping the steep to Castle View,
at the foot of the Motte, Castle Gardens lie,
sweet peace and plantings. The honeyed stroke
of gardener's craft kept sweet by growth,
greenings, flower dazzle, season's bounty, ponds.

In April the May Fayre Gathering,
with laughter and quiet spells of walk the labyrinth.
Breath hold, slowly open eyes,
emerge into wonderland of sacred space,
caring folk, poetry and song.
Maypole ribbons weaving the past into a hold of now,
patternings that grandma knew, and her grandma too.
Hands held in circle dance, painted faces, magick market.
Beyond the green, Vikings hack and slash, stories told of
myth and mayhem.
Jester singing, bladder slapping,
bells a jingling, bells a jangling into everyday,
a sense of the new, layered realms,
oasis in the mind for these unlikely times.

In August crammed with people, sun and summertime,
Family Fun Day, rubbing shoulders with the queue
for canal trips, circus skills, model engine ride
smell of burning flesh barbecue, pancakes, chips.
Squeals of children, noise of crowds drowning birdsong

for a brief while, swarming like bees in the heat.
Smiles and laughter at the clowns, the juggling,
the fire eaters, till tired out day winds home.
In between the birds claim their feeding ground,
lovers claim their benches, the dispossessed take rest,
students dally all the way, contemplate.
Along Mile Straight, swans like washing on the line,
billow by, vie with coot and moorhen,
for offered sacrificial bread.
Seasons sweep through bringing warmer and colder,
changing the park that lies
a footfall from temple ring,
a body throw from head and heel bridge.

19. IMBOLC TO MAYDAY BREAKING THROUGH

A poem inspired by newspaper articles 2nd Feb and 6th Feb 2016 'A world in one street' and 'Integration street'.

The Maypole Clock Tower reaches to the scarce sky
among the buildings,
whilst brightly clothed pedestrians
weave around the bus stops, waste bins.
Telephone boxes become portals
to other loved worlds, whilst on corners and benches
folk connect to others, interact, swap hopes.
Dancing round the central hub, leaving,
Arriving, meeting, parting, greeting,
like maypole ribbons all a flutter, folk
creating patterns, choosing directions,
spiralling, to ing and fro ing, making way
and politely pushing by, with pushchairs,
skateboards, bicycles, wheel chairs,
scooters and walking frames, shopping bags.
A world of people, dressed in every colour and style,
reminding me of the Rainbow People,
long prophesied by the Hopi, First Nation,
who dreamed that at the end of time there would arise
a people, a Rainbow Tribe, to rescue the world,
and save mankind. Is this fractured glimpse that future?
Now, swerving and swirling, this intracultural heart
of Leicester, born of its streets of splintering,
reforming, in blizzards of bodies come together
to shelter, to share, to learn from each other,
in respect, then dance their dreams
round a common hub of ribboned future,

as Spring brings a blossoming hope, even
in the city centre.

20. AUBADE

The dream of solace sleep
ebbs on the pat of paw,
morning present clawed
feather flurried down,
wakes the ear to trumpet
purr and chaffinch chit chat
of loss and fear.
Pit pat barefoot on stairs
glance at the clock
Click clack the door unlocked
creak and bang, thrown open,
stumbling onto the grass.
Hawthorn, oak, birch and yew,
buddleia, still with dew,
rustling greenery hides
distraught chirps and the tide
of challenging songs rise,
litany each morning.
I spread sunflower seeds, sing,
feel the dregs of yesterday.

21. DEMENTIA TEST

My daughter held her breath, listened,
I passed the test.
I'd read the newspaper
knew the date,
the name of the Prime Minister.
Bloods showed B12 deficiency,
a reason why, possibility
for broad brushstrokes of life drowning
in tears.
Remembrance now islands
in the breaking waves,
accessible by accident,
shipwreck triggers,
a face, music, other voices,
illuminating treasure caves,
forgotten grottos, shared space,
locust and lotus land.
Not always holding fast, nor moored tightly,
I slip away, content, enjoy
surging tidal flow sweep past leaving
the always here and now.
Memories trickling through my fingers,
or like ebb tide between my toes.
Sailing through shallow lagoons, hands hold,
Beaching, making landfall, bedrock,
hauled ashore by family, home.

2. TIME AND TIME AGAIN

1. FRIENDS
2. WELSH FIELDS
3. DELIGHT
4. IT MAYBE MAY
5. WILD STRAINED
6. BYPASS - FROM LEICESTER TO LITMARSH
7. IT'S THE LITTLE THINGS IN LIFE
8. WESTWARD WANDERER
9. HOTEL TERRACE, APRIL IN MALTA
10. PATERNOSTER
11. BOUNDARIES
12. PENELOPE'S CHILDREN WAITING FOR THE HERO TO SHOW
13. TOP TABLE
14. LOCK DOWN
15. THE BATTLE OF JUTLAND 31ST MAY 1916
16. TO JILL
17. TO ROB
18. GRIT
19. SOMETIMES BY A TEAR
20. OVER THE BRIDGE

1. FRIENDS

Sometimes we ring, sometimes we write,
sometimes we meet soul to soul,
like scattered gems in an isle of night
reflecting the gleam of eyebright dream
once shared and held as binding
in the youthful world.
Some here, some gone, some dreamed away
faded into patchwork heirlooms
of a lifesblood comfort blanket gift
of what might be, into could have been,
almost was, into look what could bloom,
deepening love into friendship's bliss,
know what is, was, might be.
Still creating worlds, dreams,
sharing.

2. WELSH FIELDS

Swirl clouds of gold dust
round about our knees,
children kicking clouds of gold
running hand in hand
through El Dorado.
Golden moments, golden dreams,
happiness, sunshine
gold dust in the wind
at El Dorado.

Buttercup fields, daisy chains
misty mountains, pastureland
sunshine falling all around
gold dust covering the ground
at El Dorado.

Pleasured pain of loss
mined deep in lonely
times when cost seems worth the gain.
Treasure still in those Welsh hills
at El Dorado.

3. DELIGHT

Delighting in play with kitten, tangled skeins
of yesterdays, stringing along with everyday.
Some times ago in Anglesey with cats, dogs,
each nurturing the all, as well as me and mine.

Hector came from the city with us
in his youth and strength, mongrel
father to pups and adopted by cats
as plaything and chase tail.

My youngsters ran and caught for cuddles,
puppies and kittens in country acres,
through cobbled yards into great
grassed fields of splattered sunbeams,
daisies and myriad places safe from see.

I never learned to knit, bought wool
instead of string, for tug of war in summer,
children versus wild spitting furballs
all quicker and seemingly more clever
than people at teasing chase.

Now, all gone, nearly faded safe from see,
back in the city with my last spitting toothless
ball of fur, she has mad moments of tease the string
before casually dropping claws, biting hard
into the soft spread of lap.
Pain renews memory of all those years,
children, puppies, kittens.

Still wondering will I ever learn to knit
a patchwork cloak
from all those tangled threads?

So much to weave, colours, meanings, you.
Easier by far to dangle tease
ends and shreds for wild young things
to guess which is tug of war, which labyrinth thread.

4. IT MAYBE MAY

Maybe I could have stayed the night
Maybe I could have joined the dance
Maybe join the wild frolics, processing
Maybe jump the flames with you
Maybe I could have seen the dawn
Maybe surrounded by revealing green
Maybe I could have seen bluebells
Maybe I could have bathed in dew
Maybe I could regret ne'er casting a clout,
Maybe felt damp breeze or Sun warmth
Maybe taken my ribbons and wove my path
Maybe listened to the wakening real world
Maybe I will go to the woods next year
Maybe then it won't be raining.

5. WILD STRAINED

Supported by the sheer strength
of logic and rethought reason
into purposeful,
will bring to growth a rough
approximation of intent.
Not full flowering but wild strained,
tempered by respect and cultivated beauty,
nurtured warmth and you.
One of all the many guides to life
and love and growing,
well met with a uniquely relevant grace in being.
The one to mark out of my bounding soul,
standards to attain, the framework to hold,
senses to be made a tune,
having the power to change worlds, words
and mainly people,
this pupil sees your world and will
step into that next dimension.
(Goodbye cruel world)
(Hello Glastonbury)

6. BYPASS – FROM LEICESTER TO LITMARSH

Since the sat-nav, the Worcester bypass
is an easier prospect.
Where once if you looked at country views
over the flood plains and lost
count of the roundabouts it was
guaranteed that a missed junction
would take ten miles in the wrong direction
before turning round and starting again.
Now we argue with the voice for several miles
before giving in graciously, being taken
on the scenic route.
Great Malvern, West Malvern, Ridgway Cross.
Alarming up-and-downs, single lanes.
Coming back it's A44, Droitwich,
Inkberrow, and Stratford.
Spinning off from the bypass,
whirligig in a lucky dip
to avoid the motorway.
Sometimes we give up, turn into Worcester
and stay for tea.

7. IT'S THE LITTLE THINGS IN LIFE

The pass is presented,
machine goes ding,
on Arriva buses
no ticket for us
O.A.P.s, Austerity
decrees we lose
that welcome check
of date and time,
the number to ring
in case of complaint
and if you were lucky
on the back a discount
for food in the warm, in town.
Now there's less litter they say
less tickets issued, more time saved
(more bemused people,
wishing for a conductor,
an inspector to talk to,
but they don't have the number
for complaints).

8. WESTWARD WANDERER

We arrived at the pick-up point Friday,
waited with a motley group of elders,
being picked on right away by a guy,
demanding to know where his partner
was taking him. He guessed Paris, romance,
hurt when the driver called out "Bristol Meads,
Steam Train to the Quantock Hills, Bath, Minehead".
Whisked away, four hours on the scenic route,
we wandered westwards, took a sneak preview
of delights of the summerlands ahead.

First toilet stop, first in, thanks to front seats.
Walking back past the queue the heady perfumes
of women in Sunday best, dressed to please,
spruced up males, gallant and mannered, in pain
but making the best of it. All determined
to have a good time, making the most use
of the journey, alone.
Snacks then a wander round Moreton-on-Marsh.
Sister Pat told me the family news,
I spoke of mine, wandering westward, home.

We stayed at a Holiday Inn, no staff
to carry our bags, forty-six halt, lame,
or blind, when the lift only holds two, alas.
We queue for food, and answer to our name.
Tables labelled "coach party", pause for thought.
Swimming pool off limits, queue for service.
Find lake, pool, fountain, rain, wind and thunder.
Four nights of luxury Hell, heat, noise, snores.
Three days of memories, inspiration.

Life stories told, understandings, wonder.

9. HOTEL TERRACE, APRIL IN MALTA

They shoot songbirds in the spring

Heat shrouded parasol poles
hunching like cowled figures
in the garden, on balcony and walkway.
Seen from below as guardians of the place,
from inside as deterrents from the heat.
Over there, part of the looked from viewpoint
to the beautiful landscape,
bleached limestone,
sea scene, of golden turquoise, ink navy,
sparkle white froth beading
the empty sands,
headland hiding more,
depriving us of the ecstatic
extension of the lovely and new.
Closer to home, yellow flowers struggling,
no birds, not even a seagull
to steal my ice-cream.

10. PATERNOSTER

Squeaky, creaky, bumpety, thud.
Chattering, clattering, squeals and grab,
jumping on as only, hand in hand or the whole gang,
jumped upon, jumped down upon
stepped gracefully, nonchalantly, tripped upon,
stepped on, leaped on, squeezed onto tightly,
over-rode and under-rode for extra excitement.
Scouting for the children and grandchildren
visiting parents. All delighting in the novelty,
proudly handed on and off, chased and collected,
delivered to the right floor, mostly.
High heels tottered, old folk lurch,
children exploring adventure with mum,
before the porter spoiled the fun, asked if we were lost?
On our way to lectures, tutorials, Mature Students Room,
mixing and meeting strangers on the Paternoster,
recognising friends and other students
not confined in blank shiny walls reflecting ourselves,
but open to the changing floors, people passing
or queueing, to shoulder to shoulder with us all,
in the Attenborough. That was Sociology in 1983.

11. BOUNDARIES

At night the creaks, tappings and squeaks increase,
until one hopes for death watch beetle.
Bathroom trips become a nightmare journey
of dappled shade, outside headlights beaming, leaving
sudden blackness chasing spider shadows,
tripping hazards reaching for tired feet
at stair top and threshold. Cord pulled, lightning
illumines cobwebs, distorting distance
to ceilings, then plunged to darkness, comfort
bright is taken back by switch and switch by
nightlight, bedside lamp scaring ghosts away.
New day, medication, I'm sudden seeming
sensitive to scurries across the floor.
Outside dancing in trees, dryads, black crow,
presences glimpsed from the corner of eye,
felt at my back, pressing for attention,
acknowledgement, familiar and new.
Boundaries conjoined, interlacing,
thin veil between the Worlds, dimensions change,
the table falls lower than the placed dish.
Suddenly the absence of guardian cat,
monitor of reality, fierce truth,
is noted, regretted, patrols of borders
undone, companion champion lost.
See glimpses of those others gone before.
The subconscious longing to know, discover,
means boundaries are seen, broken, sealed,
again and again till a path is worn
to shades in daylight, fancied unknown fears.
Overseeing plain the horrors of our world
beyond the bounds they reach out to us,

so we turn towards the light, fear the dark.
Keep boundaries clear.

12. PENELOPE'S CHILDREN WAITING
FOR THE HERO TO SHOW

The dark side of the Moon
draws down the violent and the damned,
pressing on all the wounds
of swiftflow/heartbleed/agonies
of mind stealth/warpweavings.
Slash, cut the thread (that was a stitch in time)
to unravel the accomplishment of days
spent shuttling sense into meaning
and a patterning into life.
In the timeless bound of Dark Moon
no reflection can emerge, no continuing can be seen,
just endless Now of no light at the point of no return.
No remedy but end to conscious pain
all alone in the dark.
Time to spin and dangle on the thread.
Grandmother Spider, teach me how to feel the Web,
how to sail till morning on cast off lines
of Hope, to trust in the buffeting breeze,
and tempest tossed, remain aloft.

13. TOP TABLE

Below the salt, salt of the earth,
on the Briny Deep, salt rubbed
on sore wounds, lashings,
poured in bucketsful,
decks awash in salt water,
crocodile tears, impressed,
oppressed slaves to sailing on the deep
unknown, where those grinding mills
still pour out flavouring, preserve
the tales of old sea salts.
Salt poured in herring tubs, on winter meats,
spilled salt, pinch salt
over shoulder, astral cleansing
of the working circle, tools.
Rock salt, dug deep mines,
ancient seas long gone,
left in trace and timeline
over unimagined distance.

Salt flats gleaming in a far-off haze,
distant shore, pooling turquoise,
mostly blinding white, spilling into ice
blue sky, heat trembling salt land
into mirage meld, reflected cloud
colour bright focusing into human forms,
cloth wound round head and face,
bare heels salt encrusted, red rags
protection from heat, cold, salt.
Raking, raking, raking, piling
sparkling crystals up high,
four feet high, raking, raking,

another pile, raking, raking,
four feet high, sparkling, sparkling.
Aching arms, wrinkled skin, hurting,
with salt biting deep into the wound.
Sun, glare, salt slavery, the lorry
collects twice a day, part of the process.

Even fish and chips, (loads of vinegar and salt)
binds me to known world, history, nourishment,
all those stories. Change.

14. LOCK DOWN

We locked ourselves down
taking time out to be home,
refuge in the known
watching all the screens
parading fake and true news
clinging to all views

opinions and fears
tears and anxious waiting, love
the only solace
selecting comfort
the same world view, not holding
but blowing kisses

from gargled mouths, washed
fingers across the divide
wave or clap the brave
those who do, inspire,
whilst we queue or stay at home,
distance perspective

though the 83
drives round to town gallantly
no one boards or leaves
my favoured seat waits
empty of me scribbling notes,
destination closed.

Traffic noise muted
to occasional hum of
essential journeys.
Birds calling loudly
with desperate throats unused
to filling silence.

We notice weather,
Climate change, erratic times
different dangers.
Ethnic cleansing, war,
wildlife extinction, new laws
still no protection.

Still the Government
keep us entertained with lies
and damned statistics.

Lock down.

15. THE BATTLE OF JUTLAND 31ST MAY 1916

Grandad was sunk at Jutland.
Thousands and thousands died there
in the flash and crash,
exploding mish-mash,
splash and "torpedo! ",
smoke screens and death cries,
big guns deafening,
people screaming, ships sinking,
black smoke spiralling,
fires and bucket chains,
wounded howling, men cheering
at another ship gone down.
Grandad was sunk at Jutland,
was there making history,
never once told his story.
All he ever said,
to his eldest son,
"if ever you're stuck on a sinking ship
or a badly damaged boat,
grab hold of something that floats!"

16. TO JILL

In the land of the spirit
a new lady grows to her true shape and stature.
She is welcomed. She is part.
Finding the reach and touch
of her deeds and thoughts,
she is gone, to her true path keeping.
She will ride her beloved horses
cross rainbows, galloping, waving,
she all joy, complete, welcoming,
ebullient, herself only,
all human moulding gone,
released, her shadow
ebbing from the ground before us
as tears and memory hold her shape.
She is gone, to her true path keeping,
where we will follow
as her unfolding beauty
grows to her manifest destiny.
Her meaning will touch lives
and brushes the understanding
of those like us, left to follow,
to our true paths keeping.
She will welcome us when we meet,
all paths crossing
in the lands of spirit,
where despite different costumes
we are all grown in love.

17. TO ROB

Fragile vessels all,
our lives like yours a wasting, a way.
Only shards of pleasured memory
left in the siftings
of buried, past,
painfully restored when time demands
a reckoning,
too often lost
in aware, being now.
Graffiti, wisdom, traces,
they wiped away.
Writings on a blank end wall
sometimes enhance the bleak world,
sometimes charm the soul,
some times recall.

18. GRIT

My dad was a John Wayne type of man,
a true grit man
who rarely spoke at home,
too tired from the daily grind of earn enough.
He said what he thought, a big bluff gruff man.
If he didn't actually wear six shooters
two shotguns locked in the gun cupboard
brought home rabbit and ducks in the good old days
when they were plentiful, and we girls were young.
Pretend outlaws could be dealt with, given
his self-made crossbow and the ones he gave us
with peg release triggers for practice.
He could make anything mechanical, or wooden,
he could mend anything electrical, or broken,
missed only a month from his work,
with a broken ankle, in over sixty years.
Favours, car mending for neighbours, for that
bit extra. Managing the rent, a car, the yearly holiday,
five children, mum. Never bemoaned his fate.
Villains finally came to our estate,
he quietly faced them down, made his stand,
they knew about his guns, asked to join him.
He refused to take them round local farms.
"I shoot vermin" he stated, protecting
landowners, those who let him roam their ranges
keeping down pests, treated him as equal
for his true grit ways.

19. SOMETIMES BY A TEAR

In Leicester Market, Town Hall Square,
Regeneration Road, on the benches,
on crowded buses, people from across the world,
Ghosts hidden in their eyes, let loose
sometimes by a tear, to chase us away,
sometimes by the fear of capture,
return to death.
Jostling in the Market place
their eyes hold all those flickering ghosts,
ghosts shadowing the smiles
for fond friends, safe passage,
ghosts reflected in the tears of relief
or all alone in the night time,
ghosts of family, seen in the features,
gestures, glimpses into the hollow soul.
Ghosts seen in doorways, beckoning,
Shades in alleyways, shadows behind curtains.
Repository of all Ghosts
crowding out the here and now,
demanding attention
of all their dreams.

20. OVER THE BRIDGE

The Bridge from Breakdown to Recovery

The ambulance ferried me to the bridge,
discharged me upon it.
The ringing tones of the wishes-well song
echoed healing mantra,
"Take your medication
All will be well".
The family helped me along, letting
me lean until I could walk unaided
no longer afraid of the river beneath,
glimpsed through the swinging boards
whilst hard winds blew the taut cables I clung to,
skirts swirling like a giddy
fifties rock'n'roller.
Chocolate helped. Big boxes from friends, flowers,
lots of little treats from me.
Then when the bridge settled
on firm ground, met people who didn't know,
couldn't tell, didn't hear
echoes of my healing mantra
"Take your medication
All will be well".
My daughters checked that I took all the pills.
When I was better
they let me babysit.

3. TIMES PAST

1. POTTAGE
2. LOOKING FORWARD
3. BORN INTO AUSTERITY
4. BLACK AND WHITE PHOTO
5. ANOTHER CHRISTMAS 1956
6. PERFORMANCE MEMORY 1959
7. EASTER PARADE 1958
8. THE BICYCLE
9. WHAT MY DAD TAUGHT ME
10. THE SHED SAYS IT ALL
11. KEYSTONE COPS
12. HAUNTED / GHOST IN THE MACHINE
13. DEPRESSION
14. POEM FOR TRANSGENDER REMEMBRANCE
    SERVICE
15. BIPOLAR
16. LOOK INTO MY EYES
17. SILENCE
18. WHAT I KNOW
19. SIMPLE PLEASURES
20. DANCE
21. TONY'S POEM

1. POTTAGE

Our fathers sold us
for a mess of pottage,
they were hungry.
Our brothers sold us
for a mess of profit,
they are greedy.
Mining, fishing, hunting,
fast cars, Big guns, plotting
to steal our heritage,
grasping every mote
till our eyes were blinded,
ears filled with lies.

Big guns crushing soul's
reach, big boots kick soft flesh,
trav'llers taken,
Drowned and worse.
Who now knows the way?
We bear the stench of debt,
loss, grief, and olden ways,
agony of souls squeezed,
whilst words, blatant lies,
'good intentions' twinkle
from their cunning vulture eyes,
reflect their prey,
helpless in the desert,
left behind, bereft
lonely crowds, weeping for
lost family.
Angry.

2. LOOKING FORWARD

Every month the same
looking forward, looking back,
checking the calendar
as days slide by, relentless,
tasks to do, missed, completed.
Play catch up till death releases
hold on what to do, must do,
should do, never did, whilst
the blur between the speeding
months becomes life statement,
exemplar, harvest reaped
the fruits consoling others,
rations for survival,
inspiration, continuation.
Life.

3. BORN INTO AUSTERITY

Born into a post-war prefab,
then moved onto the edge
of a newbuild council estate,
(built on a rubbish tip,
power station to the east,
Iron Works to the west,
canal beyond a flood field at the back).

We knew austerity, families of five or seven,
eleven, with ragged trousered boys,
barefoot children playing in the street,
saving their black pumps for school wear.
mothers desperately trying to dry the
soaking bedsheets for another night
of top and tailing four or more to a bed.

Times of seeing grandad crying
with the pain of blistered hands
working on the building site eleven hours a day.
Whenever I went out on the street
with a twist of brown paper hiding the sugar
and a big stick of rhubarb grown in the back yard,
I suddenly found lots of friends, wanting a lick.
Neighbours doors were always open,
you could borrow a cup of sugar,
every kid would be fed something
if there wasn't enough at home,
mostly sugar sandwiches.
But they weren't good times.

Good times came later and we'd never had it so good. I remember the man on our 6 inch black and white tele telling us so.

Even so, I don't think it was good enough.

4. BLACK AND WHITE PHOTO

On the running board
of a black Mayflower Plymouth,
white blonde hair blazing,
big smile for my dad
and his box Brownie.
"Smile our Les" he says,
grandad's car all shiny clean.
Dad looked after the machines.
Grandad in his cloth cap
worked in the greenhouse,
mom and grandma cooked.
My sisters rode horses Sunday mornings,
at the farmer's barn down the leafy lane.
Four years old, the favourite.
"Fetch this". "Take that quick to dad".
"Tell them cups of teas are here".
I'd run errands, even to the farm.
No-one to be scared of in those days.
Even by the gipsy camp,
mam would always say "don't stop,
they'll have you away"
but they never did. "Come back now" I'd say
to the girls, riding.
Back to the family, reality, long ago,
shown and remembered,
that black and white photo.

5. ANOTHER CHRISTMAS 1956

4am we woke, saw bulging socks hung on the door,
all Santa's mince pies and milk gone.
We'd peered through the shared frosting window,
across the estate, past the power station and iron works
into the mainly sky, for trace of Rudolph's red nose
or galloping hooves or someone jumping down
chimneys.
Hugged each other for warmth, and slept.
Now despite the clouding breath
and cold toes we only paused to check
the names on the card in each sock,
before dragging our prizes back to the bed.
Hidden deep inside dad's best black socks
were oranges, nuts, gloves, and chocolate coins
covered in gold, tied in a string, apples and satsumas.
Jacqui and I ate 'til our noses grew cold, started to drip
then back under the bedclothes to sleep.
Mum called us at eight when the fire was lit.
Downstairs in our dressing gowns, all four girls had
pillowcases.
Mine was the best ever: Treasure Island, Famous Five,
Little Women,
slippers, drawing book and pencils, needlework and silks,
but best of all
a wind-up Cinderella that spun around her ballroom
on the lino I polished every Saturday.
Our once-a-year chicken and stuffing for dinner.
The Queen's speech.

6. PERFORMANCE MEMORY 1959

Every year the cards reinforce the memory
of that last year, that last year in the juniors.
I was the chosen one, dressed in a blue robe.
I danced for joy when Rachel / Gabriel told me
the good news. I trekked heavily towards the stable
and the finale. As the donkey plodded round,
I laid the baby in the manger and posed,
golden-haired amongst the angels,
whilst the three kings brought their blessings.
On-looking teachers were so impressed
by my skill and passion, that next year
as a senior, I was asked back
to reprise the role for a dark-haired
would-be Mary, who couldn't dance in her soul.

7. EASTER PARADE 1958

All year round I wore hand-me-downs,
at Easter mum bought me new clothes;
Coat, hat, shoes, sometimes gloves and dress
(Provident club card, bob a pound).
Nine years old, I choose a scarlet
red swing coat, that flowed round my knees,
hid the ground, rippled, as I walked.
Reminded me of poppies, bright sunsets.
The coolie hat of white straw, net,
red spots, red trim, like a lampshade,
curved to deflect, pointed like a pyramid.
Tied under chin, I felt really old.
I was so chic, modern, fifties, cool.
Matching gloves (like debutantes) added class,
whilst patent black shoes mirrored me.
Walking free from the shop I swirled, flowed.
Danced like Cinderella.

8. THE BICYCLE

Over the years, clanking chain, skipping gears,
slippy handles and bottom bruising seat.

My mother's bicycle, sit-up-and-beg,
with rattling chain, three gears to help up hills,
a black framed steed, with front willow basket,
handbag, shopping, found flowers, children's treats,
gloves,
and her rounds list, payment books held secure.

She'd say "when you can reach the pedals then
I'll teach you to ride". Day after day, home
from school, I'd see mum's bike waiting for me,
under the window, or in the entry
as she prepared the evening meal.

Leaning on the wall, scrabbling up to sit,
my legs dangled feet closer and closer,
my arms stretched, held my spine straight, tippy toes
reached the floor, one foot on the top pedal.

Mum took me out to learn. The bike was kind.
Legs covered in greasy oil - school clothes ruined.
Morning and evening, sweet simple machine,
you served on mother's rounds, club collector.

Weekday afternoons you were my best friend,
we could explore, travel for miles,
in hours away from the power station,
away from glue factory, iron foundry.
We found the big park, waste ground, school friends, but

most of all you and I found adventure.

Clanking chain, skipping gears, slippy handles,
bottom bruising seat, pedals bruising legs.

Holding tightly to your rubber hand grips
we were steered towards discovery.

A spoil heap 'mountain' beyond sprawling houses
led me to push you with bouncing wheels to
the very top. I left you there, black frame
nestling amongst the flowering gorse bushes,
saddle empty, wheels spinning loosely.

My faithful steed, guarding and waiting.
Drawn by the vision of turquoise water
in the old quarry with almost-island
lit by the orange glow of an afternoon sun,
I felt like a Famous Five or Secret
Seven, or perhaps a Terrific Two.
You took me safely home again after
each adventure. Dad repaired you and then
we'd set out again.

Clanking chain, skipping gears, slippy handles,
and bottom bruising seat.

9. WHAT MY DAD TAUGHT ME

He taught one sister to drive.
Another to work with dogs.
I was left, the middle one of five girls,
between two stillborn sons, always a vague
disappointment.
Then when mum died, he showed how much he loved
me
by teaching me the secret of a perfect cup of tea.
Fourteen days before the funeral for me to try and fail
to recreate just as he asked, that brew that only he
and mum shared before. Two weeks of
constant criticism, ridicule and tears, tea being
thrown away, discarded, sipped once and spat out.
He made fun of me and my incompetency.
In the kitchen – suddenly different with
no tobacco smoke and open windows – he taught me
how to replace mum in one degree,
gifted the secret of tea making for the perfect cup of tea.
Squeezing out the teabags exactly three and a half
minutes
after the water splashed down.
Wait, wait, ready now,
adding a dash of sterilized milk to tannin brown,
sweetening the burnt taste with two and a half scoops of
white
twinkling sugar on the right spoon, stirring slowly.
All of it worth the the stress. On the day of the funeral,
mournfully trying to cope and be strong for all us
weeping relatives,
four or five times throughout the day
"Make us a cup of tea, our Les". Just right. Perfect.

10. THE SHED SAYS IT ALL

Along the path, up six steps, there's the shed,
wrapped in roofing felt and dad's private space.
Weeds at foundations, past tensions unsaid.
Unwashed windows at his once special place,
butt outside flows onto mum's flower bed.

No plugs plugged, stale sawdust on the floor,
the lathe on safety, the block we stood on
making stools, cots, go-karts, doll's houses and more
whilst he helped us shape future play, long gone.
Footsteps in the sawdust. Mask behind door.

11. KEYSTONE COPS

In the fusty musty
flea pit thruppenny seats,
shabby and unsprung in
the run down Odeon,
full of kids,
on Saturday mornings
screaming, laughing
at the screen,
black and white life
illumined by screen light,
everyone with someone
Not me, (sisters too old or too young
to adventure).
Popcorn escaping as pocket money hands
shook with excitement
feeding the scramble for free food.
Black and white flashes and glare
Episodes of Keystone Cops,
running after, being dragged,
hit by traffic or comrades
seemingly oblivious to the plight
of the less fortunate amongst them,
focused on duty or the road ahead.
I never found funny in slapstick,
anxiety and sympathy for hurts
endured, ensured I never laughed.
Years later coloured films were shown,
Lassie was relief, nature film shorts
bliss, true escapism
until sitting in the stalls
a lad spat into my plaits

from the balcony above.
I never went again, spent Saturdays
and every day seeing life as
black and white.

12. HAUNTED/GHOST IN THE MACHINE

those animals stood
like a mirage in the heat
wavering in flame

those humans float by
flotsam and jetsam on tides
no profit no help

on the shore, tangled
feathers, skulls and whales, beached,
ghost rigging, plastic

on the far mountain
bombs blossom, volcanos roar
Fate of the world, now

view from the dead Tree
snaking toward Tor, Stonehenge,
roads cleaving history

view the populace
via newspaper headlines
doomed races doomed places

shreds of hope cling on
to barbed wire, floating dreams, love,
haunting nightmares, ghosts.

Then we stay at home.
Wildlife thrives, pollution's pall
lifts, shows a green world.

Life returns
fewer folk to harm the earth.
What goes on unchecked?
Economic exceptions,
HS2 clearing old woods
National Trust sells out
Stonehenge to tourists,
shale fields bought on line,
country hidy holes
for rich folk, politicians
dealing harm to each and all.

No green economy,
profit, for the addicted
to more, more and more.

Careful what you wish for,
wish for sun, sun will come,
karmic law, fingers burn.
Then Change comes.

13. DEPRESSION

The chasms of despair loom deeply,
Unaware of the future depths of reach,
Slipping hands held for moments,
The comfort of (perhaps) escape
From the unending slide toward
Uncomfortable oblivion of once secure.
The anguished letting go
Or the 'passioned desperate clutch
Of double drowning, dealt as joker.
Half wild in ecstasy,
Half crazed with pain,
Drowning sense in lost and found,
Come to (nought)
And the glad leap
Or the sad slip,
Intent or accident
Result is still the same.
Hit the rocky bottom,
Roll (almost right) up again.
Each timed to a further and a less gone.

14. POEM FOR TRANSGENDER REMEMBRANCE SERVICE

Some fears, the boogyman under the stairs,
the Troll beneath the Bridge,
the knock on the door in the night-time,
never go away.
Bad dreams on waking,
never go away.

The layerings of fear and hurt resonate
into the now, into the memory
created by a careless touch, a hate filled word,
never goes away,
hides in silence, though
never goes away.

Some fears, the greatest fears of all alone,
all alone in the world,
of starting afresh and being done down
never go away
until a hand reaches to hold on tight,
a voice is glad to have found you and speaks
from the heart of love
"You will never be alone".

15. BIPOLAR

Emerging from the medication shroud,
parts of me run to the extremes
of thought and imagine,
behaving in ways that alarm
those not used to the restless
travelling, (doomed to repeat
the alarm, "Have you had your Pills?").
Taken away in the moment,
the intense focus on making
surfaces clean, stammering, slurred
speech and totally different priorities.
Sparkly spending's,
great joy, confidence and the spark
of enthusiasm, give way
to waves of darkness, horror, pain.
Incentive: to take the medicine again.

16. LOOK INTO MY EYES

Look into my eyes.
Seen there amongst the unveiled wisdoms,
naked seventeen, Solstice summering in day-glo.
Nineteen, casting body majicks with the sea,
spelled to the powers of overload.
Beswirling twenties outreached time
and stood still the eternities.
Seeing happy, sadness, love touched pain,
along with all those used-to beings
met along the chosen path.
Gloried furies of the thirties
checked and seen in elemental form,
known depths the springboard
from frightened child and tied.
Your eyes reflect the shadows
fleeing from your gaze,
shriven by the blaze
of finger strummed vibration
shaking to the deepest reach
of heightened sense and joy.
The trembling tumbled imagery
shakes loose once hallowed, enshrined
hold, illumined in a clarity
of visioning, fired by bolts of truth.
Crushes shadows, crumbles to the dust of ages old.
Sweet zephyred kiss blows.

17. SILENCE

Apologies to john cage 4 minutes 33 seconds

In between the announcements,
silence calls to everyone,
then, "Ticket number 9, please go to the counter".
Flutters of ticket holders checking tickets
for the umpteenth time.
Someone rises, departs. The silence falls again.

The silence when a child stops crying.
That damp, sticky silence and hopefully sleep.
Tiptoe quiet "Shush now, quiet. Bedtime."

The silence when snow falls and birds hide
after the footfall and snowball squelch,
the silence when the window slams shut on the noisy
road.
The silence when teacher asks "who knows the
answer?".
The silence when the last night bus is gone,
city centre empty 'til cleaners come.

That special filled up silence in revered place or space.
That shushes intruders, then welcomes them in.
The shared silence of respect while remembering.
The silence of a fugitive when hiding.

The silence of an audience before curtain-up,
wondrous sounds that fill the absence
like filigree fingers soaring through the mind,
conjuring the potential of music to fill silence.

The silence that expects all expectation be fulfilled.

18. WHAT I KNOW

I know when life is hard, times are grim.
I know my cat loves me, he claws and paws
(keep those purrs coming, they drown out the world).
I know I'm privileged, I eat regular.
I know how to wash up, know how to clean.
I know what I was like before the pills.
I know the brutalities that beat us down.
I know my fear of being on my own
    (with all my memories or none).
I know when the seasons turn.
    Celebrate eight times a year.
I know what principles and beliefs
    I can hold to, before I break.
I know how to keep a man happy
    (enough to stay).
I know my bus pass could take me travelling.
I know my family and love is there.
I know how to be quiet and still
    (I was a life model in another life).
I know that no news is good news most times.
I know not to bring more violence
    and unkindness into the world.
I know three times back for all you give
    should be the rule.
I know constant learning sharpens the mind.
I know I'll never remember it all.
I know not everyone can be trusted
    sometimes what I know is perfect trust.
I know not everyone can love.
I know my beloved cares for me.
    Perfect love.

19. SIMPLE PLEASURES

Soft sighs of wonder, beauty in the world anew
In the garden seeing bumble bee's journey
May day rising to wash in dawn dew
Planning the day, clearing the screen
Limiting puzzles to a time lost looking for solutions
Every day caught by the cat for strokes and play
Family visits, hugs and kisses
Feeding birds, rewarded in song.

Pleasure of your hand in mine when we walk
Leaving with the bus pass, a return journey
Easing into old routines still valid
Answering the phone, knowing who calls
Still dancing to tunes we've danced for years
Understanding the diagnosis
Remembering the directions
Ending the day at home
Snuggling under fresh sheets at night
In love's company.

20. DANCE

The mating dance of the red-crowned crane
most beautiful of all,
reaffirming the bonding,
parting and joining,
spinning, delicately stepping.
Repeated every bedtime at ten pm,
we rise hand in hand,
tiptoe up the stairs.
We rise hand in hand,
flushed from cover by
the ending of the play on TV.
Opening the bathroom door,
we turn into stilted cranes,
treading to the water bowl.
Heads turn sideways
to each other and back
to face the mirror self.
Elderly birds in practised
ballet moves.
Hands flap up to the toothpaste shelf.
Elbows bend to brush the teeth.
Jigsaw placements of accessories
lifted, replaced as we step past each other.
Find the towel, duck under arm,
brush against each other. Turn the tap,
fill the glass, heads turn and bob
and shake. Under outstretched arm
turn and swish like stilted cranes,
chin tips towards the ceiling,
gargling, eyes narrowed,
we step gingerly

take turns to spit, swill, swish;
hang towels to soften the walls.
A leap toward the door,
mock bow and wave on,
mock curtsey, then run before,
flicking lights out on the way.
Arms caress and stroke and hold,
slide and squeeze and flutter,
swoop, settle and nest.
Peck, peck, brush heads gently,
circle into sleep, life's outer edges.
Elderly stilted cranes.
Fragile but still dancing.

21. TONY'S POEM

I told my beloved,
"children, grandchildren, cats first"
in my heart, true loves.

All grown, gone from home
I see your steadfast love
mirrors mine for you.

Long hair, - white from care,
troubled times and hope,
sign of times weathered,
your badge of freedom,
joy, measure of years, -
tumbles on pillows.

Savouring pleasure
precious human, being all,
holding, embracing.
Gifting our treasures
gleaned from past and present lives
to nurture our shared future.

Passing on our tales of adventure
togetherness, tenderness, all,
in words and deeds, keeping on.
Keeping on.

Life is a series of experiential adventures – shaping the spirit.

About The Author

Lesley Clary Sage is a Green Pagan, poet, protester, Tarot counsellor and community activist. Originally from Walsall, before relocating to Leicester, she enjoys playing an active role in the diverse and intracultural nature of the city, organising not for profit festivals, Maypole dancing, poetry and music events, health fairs, and Pagan Ceremonies. In 1995, triggered by an abusive relationship, Lesley was diagnosed as bipolar. Since then, she has been on a creative journey in which she found solace through the art of poetry, spirituality, and the support of her family.

Printed in Great Britain
by Amazon